The Tale of Three Coaches

Ask and bask. Tell, farewell!
- Daren Martin

Acknowledgements

Thank you to all of the executives, managers, and supervisors, I have worked with over the years that modeled excellent leadership skills as well as those from whom I learned what not to do.

Pregame

This book idea came to me after struggling to help a manager understand the difference between coercion and influence. I talk to countless managers who bemoan the fact that their people are "just not motivated". I question whether this is the case. Even the hardcore union worker who seems to have little interest in his or her job expresses significant motivation about other interests (their bowling league or bass fishing). They may even show a significant amount of motivation at work when it comes to "fighting the system."

I am convinced all people are motivated. A skilled manager looks for ways to invite players to get their head in the game. Systems either encourage genuine interest or discourage it. Management styles either motivate or de-motivate passion and energy.

What seems to get quick results on the front end (coercion, bribery, or threats) seldom has lasting results or impact. In addition, you give up influence overtime until you end up like the manager who was described with this comment: "There isn't a person in this place that would do a damn thing for that guy!"

This brief book invites you into the locker room of three different teams with three different coaches. Each of the three coaches wants to succeed. They all want to win a championship. They, however, have different motivations and use different tactics to motivate their team.

This book is a quick read on your own, but is even more effective when read as a team. Use the questions at the end of each chapter to spark discussion and provoke thought.

The Tale of Three Coaches

Championship Motivation

Daren K. Martin, PhD

Table of Contents

The Meeting 3

Camp 19

Game One 33

Post Season 47

Conclusion 62

Daren Martin

If you want to build a ship, don't drum up people together to collect wood and don't assign them tasks and work, but rather teach them to long for the endless immensity of the sea.

– Antoine de Saint-Exupery

Leadership is the capacity to translate vision into reality.

– Warren Bennis

The first responsibility of a leader is to define reality.
The last is to say thank you. In between, the leader is a servant.

– Max Depree

THE MEETING

*Great leaders engage hearts,
poor ones direct hands.*

– Daren Martin

Coach Johnson

"Yes, I understand". Dave Johnson hung up the phone, took a deep breath and walked into the locker room where his team was gathered. There is something about seeing a seven foot dude in front of a big screen with his paws dwarfing a video game controller that reminds you where you are.

"Okay guys, huddle up". The players slowly pull away from what they are doing and gather in the center of the room.

Coach Johnson clears his throat and starts...

"There is no doubt that we had a bad year last year. Hell, we have had a bad 4 years. I just got off the phone with our owner who chewed me a new one. He issued a mandate. What he said in so many words is we either get a lot closer to a championship this year or I am gone as a head coach and chances are, most of you are gone as well. He is tired of supporting a losing team and the pressure is on. So we either figure out how to make some serious progress from our below 500 season last year or it is lights out. Now let's get down to work."

"For starters, I am going to need all of you at camp two weeks early this year." The room erupts with groans. "Look!" Coach Johnson bellows, "I don't like it either but I'm not going to lose my job because you guys don't want to work hard."

A hand shoots up, "Yes Horst". "Coach, we sucked last year, how can you expect us to go from losing most of our games to seriously chasing a championship, that is ridiculous!" Coach Johnson responds, "Hey, it's not me, I am just telling you that our jobs are on the line. If you want to keep playing for this team you better figure out how to get it done." More groans. "Anymore questions? Okay, I will see you in two weeks at camp, early! Come prepared to win."

The team slowly makes their way out of the locker room, heads hung low. Dave

Johnson looks around the empty locker room, turns off the lights, and then walks out himself.

Coach Jackson

Coach Jackson entered the locker room with deliberation. Four losing seasons in a row had taken their toll and it was time for a change. He was fed up and felt like the time off had provided an epiphany of sorts. Despite the record, he was a winner and he was ready to start winning. The chatter slowly died down as Keith Jackson motioned for silence.

"Listen up guys, I am sick of being on a losing team. I am sick of hanging my head when I run into other coaches and players from this league. I am tired of being the laughing stock of our conference. I don't have much longer in my prime as a head coach and I want to win and I want to win this year. Now you are either on board or not but I am going to do whatever it takes to get the championship for which I have worked all my career."

The coach's eyes scan the room in anticipation of what is coming next. Players look at the coach and each other quizzically sensing that what's about to come next can't be good for them.

"That starts with you guys showing up to camp two weeks early this year." "You've got to be kidding" one of the plays mutters under his voice in the midst of audible sighs. "Complain all you want", says Jackson, but that is the way it is going to be. You either cooperate or I will make your life a living hell this year. I am serious about this and I need you to support me." "There go my vacation plans mutters Jim Jenkins (everyone calls him "Jenks") to anyone within whisper range.

"And that's not all," continues coach Jackson, "you better be in shape when you get to camp or you will be fighting for your position. Now go get your house in order and come back in a few weeks ready to work your rears off or suffer the consequences. Any questions? Good. Let's go".

Coach Tenley

Dean Tenley woke from his sleep with a start. He glanced at the clock, 3 am. The tension had been mounting all week as he anticipated the start of a new season. What would he tell his guys? There was increasing pressure from the owner and the media criticism had grown to a loud and persistent din. The chatter at the sports bars was about this team, <u>his</u> team's losing record. He got up, splashed his face with cool water from the sink, grabbed his note pad and pen and settled into his favorite chair. In the dim light he wracked his brain wondering what to say to his team. What would inspire and motivate them, ... what could possibly make a difference?

Walking into the locker room 6 hours later the note pad was still empty. "Okay guys, gather around". Slowly the players assembled. "Look", he started, "I know last year and the previous three years are a big disappointment. I wouldn't be truthful if I said that the consistent losing is not starting to take a toll on me. But more importantly, what grieves me is I look around and see defeat in your faces. I sat up all night trying to think of something inspirational, something clever to say that may jumpstart this team but for the life of me, the words wouldn't come." Mike, the "star" point guard, looks at the ceiling as if to say, "I wish you had found the words." "The only thing I know" Coach Tenley continues "is that we are in this together." We are a team and whatever happens we will celebrate or suffer through it together. So I ask you, what do you want to see happen this year?"

They say silence is golden but it feels like an eternity before the ten year veteran and center Kevin Jordan speaks up. "All I know is I am tired of losing. I remember when I first joined this team" he continues, "we could hold our head high in the community, we had respect, fans loved us. Now I am lucky if I make it out at dinner without being ridiculed or disrespected in some way." Heads hang low from other players who obviously shared this experience. Other players chime in with stories of how losing is impacting them.

Coach Tenley refocuses the group. "So if you don't like losing I ask you again, what do you want to see happen this year?" Mike chimes in, "Well that's easy coach, I want to win for a change." "Talk about that" says Coach Tenley, "Why and what would winning look like?" "Well for starters" Mike says, "all that disrespect would go away...but you know, forget other people, I would be able to start respecting myself again." Several heads nod. "Who else would like to win this year?" Slowly hands go up until they are all raised.

"Will wanting to win make it happen?" Coach Tenley asks. There is silence but every player knows the answer to that question. Wishing never got anybody anything. "So what is it going to take?" Coach asks. "Well for starters, we have to quit thinking like losers," mumbles Callahan the power forward.

"He's right" a second year rookie chimes in. "Good, what else?" asks Coach Tenley. "Well, we are going to have to work a lot harder, I think we all know the areas we have to improve if we want to win," says Kevin. "What would working harder look like?" Coach Tenley asks. "Well, maybe we cut our break short and show up early to camp...I mean, I heard the Lions did that last year and they ended up playing for the championship..." quips one of the players. At first there is resistance to this idea as players contemplate their already made plans but the idea quickly gains steam until there is unanimous consensus. "What else?" Coach asks. "Well, we need a plan" one of the more quiet players offers. "Good point" affirms Coach Tenley. "Yeah, and we all have to be in agreement that we are going to pursue this, no slacking allowed." "Absolutely, we are either all in or it is not going to work."

By the time the meeting finishes several action steps are agreed to. The team will reconvene two weeks early for training camp. In the meantime, several players volunteer to meet with the coach on a daily basis to draft a strategy for success. All team members agree to define why they want to win and to bring their statement to camp with them to share with the whole group.

Questions:

- Describe the style of each of the coaches.

- How will the players feel leaving each of these meetings? What will they be thinking?

- What is the difference between an idea the team comes up with and one imposed on them by their coach?

- How will each of these teams show up for camp?

- How motivated will they be to perform?

- How effective will the coach be at motivating his team?

- Which coach more closely resembles your or your manager's style?

NOTES

_____

_____

_____

_____

_____

_____

_____

_____

_____

_____

_____

_____

_____

_____

_____

_____

_____

_____

_____

_____

_____

_____

Daren Martin

A leader is a dealer in hope.

Napoleon Bonaparte

Become the kind of leader that people would follow voluntarily; even if you had no title or position.

Brian Tracy

Camp

*"Our" plan trumps "my" plan
every time.*

– Daren Martin

Team Johnson

"Where's Horst" coach asks. "He'll be here, he said he may not make it until the morning because he is wrapping up some stuff " responds one of the players. "Who else is missing?" A quick headcount reveals four missing players all but one who sent some kind of "I'll be late" message through a teammate. "Great" coach mutters sarcastically. "Just so you know, I am keeping track of who is committed or not... the owner is serious about wanting to know where the dead weight is."

"We're going to start by getting back in shape." (Audible groaning). Some of you look like you camped out at the Krispy Kreme all off-season. Laughter erupts as several players high five and compare their belly jiggles to see who wins. " In addition, we are going to work on learning a new system. "Coach!" complains Richard the six-year veteran. "We just really learned the last one! A new system is going to take a lot of time!" "Why do you think we came two weeks early?" coach Johnson asks in exasperation.

"Listen guys", coach continues, "I don't necessarily like it anymore than you do, but keep in mind what is at stake here. If you like playing professional ball, at least on this team, you better get your attitude straightened out or none of us will be here come next year."

"With this new system we should at least score more and look good in the process. Maybe we will get lucky and win more than we lose." Coach Johnson goes to the board and begins describing several new elements to their game plan. Horst, walking in late, stares at the board and then blurts out, "What is this? Not another new system!?" "Listen Horst" reprimands Coach Johnson, "you have a lot of nerve walking in here late and complaining. This IS a new system and you WILL learn it... or not play!" Several players snicker. Their knowing glances acknowledge the idle threat. Coach has to play their big forward if they are to have any chance of winning... bad attitude or not.

The meeting seems to last forever. Several bored players position themselves so they can play on their phones behind the cover of other players. Eventually Coach Johnson concludes his monologue and the players disperse.

Team Jackson

"Okay, I need your full attention" the team meeting is starting three hours late as they had to wait for some of the key players to arrive. "I spent the last two weeks drafting a strategy and a game plan that I think will get us where I want to go." Now, it's very different from what we have been running so I need your full commitment to learning it. Obviously, that is going to require practicing all day and studying at night." Players groan audibly.

Coach Jackson continues, "Pick up your packets off the table, they have the new system outlined. In addition, there is a log for you to track the amount of time you spend studying and also your work out time, I want to see who is working and who is not." Several players roll their eyes at the room when they are sure Coach Jackson can't see them. Responding to the log, one of the players mutters a little too loudly, "We're not kids you know". Coach Jackson, growls back, "Well until you can prove otherwise, that is exactly how you will be treated."

Sheepishly one of the players ventures "Coach, we're not running that aggressive system we toyed with a few years back are we?" "Why?" coach asks, "We had some success with that system." "Yes but... we got pretty banged up underneath and had more injuries than usual..." Coach glares at the player with the audacity to question his plan. "And your point is...?" he asks, after what seems like an eternity to the player in the hot seat. The player shrugs and dips his head. "Anymore stupid questions?" the coach continues. "Great, lets get to work."

Coach Jackson takes out his cell phone, hits speed dial and walks out of the room. Grudgingly the players line up to get their "assignments."

Team Tenley

Anticipation fills the air as the last player to arrive walks in almost an hour before the scheduled meeting time. Several players huddle and compare notes of the ideas they have compiled for getting off to a good start. One player analyzed all their losses the previous year and listed bullet points of what went wrong and what they will need to fix to keep it from happening this year. Other players take turns showing of their "guns" and describing how they had beefed up their workout to gain their trophies. Other players sit quietly reflecting on the year to come.

Coach Tenley walks confidently into the room warmly greeting and shaking the hands of his players as he enters. The buzz quiets as coach Tenley walks to the center of the room. The player's eyes are glued to their coach in anticipation. "If I look a little tired", he starts, "it's because I haven't gotten much sleep the last few weeks mapping out a new system that might actually work for this motley crew". The accompanying wide grin causes the players to erupt in laughter.

"Seriously," he continues, "I had quite a bit of help from several of you and I think we may be on to something but we are going to need the involvement, input, and buy in of everyone in this room. It's a pretty aggressive system but should take the other teams by surprise at least early on and give us a chance to jump out of the gate quick. It's going to require both brain and lots of brawn. It is key that we have each other's backs so we need to know the system like the back of our hands. The risk for injury could increase with this kind of play so I want to make sure we are all in agreement that this is the way we want to go." The room is a little quiet until Callahan quips, "You're talking about us injuring our opponents right?" The players erupt once more into laughter with high fives and shouts of bravado quickly filling the room. "If we play it right, they will be the ones on the bad end of the deal," Coach Tenley continues.

"So let's get started!" one of the player jumps in almost interrupting. Several other players chime in saying, "Yeah, lets roll", "We're ready coach!" Coach Tenley exclaims, "That's what I want to hear. Let's get started."

He goes to the board and starts outlining a quick overview of the "Win Strategy". The players are interested, attentive, and most take notes. They work diligently through lunch with sandwiches being brought in so they can keep talking about the new system while they eat. At one point Coach Tenley breaks them up into teams asking them to talk openly about what they have heard. He tells them he wants every group to come back with a list of recommendations to improve the system. The teams dive in with gusto. In the debrief time several really great ideas come out. Coach Tenley enthusiastically takes notes while verbally applauding the ones suggesting them.

At the end of a long day something uncharacteristic to this team happens. They decide in mass to go to dinner together. In previous years, little pockets of friends would always jet out of the practice facility heading for different areas. This team was starting to gel.

Questions:

- What were the differences in preparation among the teams?

- What are some things that accounted for this difference?

- How will the moods in the various meetings drive performance?

- What is the difference between "my strategy" and "our strategy"? How does it impact performance and engagement?

- How important is planning and preparation in a business setting?

- In your organization is planning a top down phenomenon or a team event with engaged involvement of all players?

NOTES

_____

_____

_____

_____

_____

_____

_____

_____

_____

_____

_____

_____

_____

_____

_____

_____

_____

_____

_____

_____

_____

_____

My own definition of leadership is this: The capacity and the will to rally men and women to a common purpose and the character which inspires confidence.

—*General Montgomery*

Leadership is lifting a person's vision to high sights, the raising of a person's performance to a higher standard, the building of a personality beyond its normal limitations.

—*Peter Drucker*

Game One

I work harder with you than for you.

– Daren Martin

Team Johnson

The players pace nervously in anticipation of their first real game of the year. Preseason had been mediocre at best. They won about 40% of their games but even the ones they won did not bode well for the coming season. Several players are nursing injuries and listed as tentative for game one. Coach Johnson has been in regular contact with the owner who continues to apply pressure and give frequent subtle and not so subtle reminders about Coach Johnson's future with the team if they don't put a winning season together.

Coach Johnson seems distracted as the starters circle up minutes before the game is to begin. "Alright, this is it. Hopefully our work will prove effective tonight. Remember I want to see scoring, not showboating, points on the board! Lets try to come out strong and who knows, maybe we can take game one."

"Any questions?" Coach Johnson asks? "None? Okay, well get out there and let me see what you got." The players drift out on the court taking their positions for tip off.

8 Minutes into the game, they trail by 8. The team looks relatively uninspired and flat. Doug makes a mental error and ends up inbounding the ball to the wrong team. Coach Johnson calls a time out and confronts Doug while the other players grab water, "What were you thinking!?" "Coach" says Doug, "I ran the play like you designed it!" "No you didn't Doug!" Coach Johnson retorts. "The play I designed and called moves left not right where *you* threw the ball!" "Have you not studied at all?" "Of course I have coach but there is just a lot to keep up with. "Whatever, hit the bench", says a weary Coach Johnson. One of the players hears him mutter, "It's going to be a long season." as he walks by.

They end up losing by 14 in a disappointing and mediocre performance. Coach Johnson makes a few perfunctory comments in the locker room then dismisses the team.

His phone is already ringing, as he is last to leave. It's the owner and the conversation is brief. "I know, I know….yes… we're trying to. I'll be there first thing in the morning." He hangs up the phone and says to no one "And to think this used to be fun."

Coach Jackson

Coach Jackson bursts into the locker room. "Alright guys, I need your best, this first game is going to indicate to me where your heads and hearts are for this season. Quite frankly, I was very disappointed in our preseason. Even though we split wins and losses, I am still not confident you are going to get me where I am trying to go. I am serious about this being a good year for me. "Me?" one of the players questions. "You know what I mean", mumbles coach Jackson... "us".... "So get out there tonight and show me some good reason I shouldn't replace the whole lot of you."

The players file out to the court and methodically begin their pre-game warm ups. "Inspirational huh?" remarks fast Jim to one of the rookies as he lumbers by. "Yeah, really pumped me up," mutters the rookie. Jim pauses for a second then remarks, "Well I'll tell you one thing, I am not going to be left holding the bag." Win or lose, I WILL get mine! If I have a great year maybe I can get traded off this worthless team and finally have a crack at a championship ring." The players bump fists.

At half time they are 4 points behind. They have stayed in the game but it hasn't been pretty. On court bickering early on divided the team and they seemed to be competing with each other half the time. Jim was hot and hitting a lot of his shots but had also forced a number of lame shots that would have been perfect assist opportunities. Several of the other players expressed their frustration through eye rolling and muttered comments. Jim just shrugged his shoulders and kept grabbing the ball every chance he got.

Somehow, the other team goes flat and Coach Jackson gets his win. The locker room afterwards is more tense than celebratory. Coach Jackson debriefs the game, which consists mainly of picking apart their play and chiding them about needing more from them. He closes by saying, "The one bright spot, Jim, 28 points, now that's what I want to see!" Jim beams, but there is very half-hearted applause from the rest of the team.

As soon as Coach Jackson finishes, the players bolt.

Coach Tenley

The players gather in the locker room. There is a calm quiet that permeates the room. The 50% win loss record in the preseason wasn't as good as anyone would have liked but the good news was most of the losses were early on and they were entering the regular season on a four game winning streak. Besides, the losses yielded valuable information and the team was starting to get the hang of using their losses to make the necessary adjustments.

"You guys have worked really hard in the pre-season and I am immensely proud of you. This season is a marathon not a sprint. No matter what happens tonight I will be pleased if I see your best and if you grow as a player and a team. Kevin bellows, "Oh, we're going to win coach!" The room erupts with enthusiastic responses. Coach Tenley, grins, "Well stick to what we have practiced and learned and I have no doubt we can take home the win."

There is some last minute strategizing. Players quickly review the game plan and share intel with each other about the other team. There is a steady confidence as they file out of the locker room. Once on the court a couple of the players start tag teaming one of the other teams rookies with disparaging comments to tear down his confidence. He ignores them but you can tell it is getting to him. Coach Tenley's players wink at each other and keep up the tirade.

They are off to a slow start but make some necessary adjustments and assault the other team with precision offense and fierce defense. Going into half time they are up by

8. They are fatigued from the full throttle effort but are starting to get in a rhythm and are even having a little fun.

The locker room is abuzz with analyzing the first half as each player is eager to throw in his 2 cents about what they saw, including weaknesses to exploit, and opportunities to seize. Finally coach Tenley has to

Daren Martin

take charge of the conversation and start to combine the observations into a coherent 2nd half plan. The players are eager to get back on the court.

102-96 is the final score with Tenley's team coming out on top. The players are exuberant but steady. There is a celebratory attitude in the locker room but also a sober realization that the season is just starting. Coach Tenley congratulates the team being careful to make specific observations about great individual efforts. He saves the highest accolades for the team play, cooperation, and synchronization that he witnessed. Spirits are high as they leave the locker room. Most of the players decide to grab a late much earned meal together before heading home.

Questions:

- How is preparing mentally for something different from preparing physically? Which is more important?

- What tools did the different coaches use to attempt to get the outcome they desired?

- How does building team performance differ from building individual performance?

- When your team goes to battle or faces game day how confident are you in their willingness and ability to stick together?

- What do you or your manager do to prepare your team for victory?

NOTES

_____

_____

_____

_____

_____

_____

_____

_____

_____

_____

_____

_____

_____

_____

_____

_____

_____

_____

_____

_____

_____

A leader is best when people barely know he exists, when his work is done, his aim fulfilled, they will say: we did it ourselves.

—*Lao Tzu*

People buy into the leader before they buy into the vision.

—*John Maxwell*

Earn your leadership every day.

—*Michael Jordan*

Post Season

We beats me.

– Daren Martin

Team Johnson

Somehow Coach Johnson's has managed to make it into the playoffs as a wildcard. They have struggled on and off all year. Flashes of really good play have been riddled with stretches of mediocre to very poor play. Fortunately, their division is not very competitive so they managed to edge out a couple of even worse teams and make it out of the regular season. As the playoff picture unfolds they discover that they are going to have to play one of the best teams in the league in the first round. Several of the players secretly schedule their vacation plans for days after the first round will be over.

Coach Johnson is increasingly stressed as he tries to hold the team together. Several camps have emerged and it becomes evident that a few of the players would like to make a run for it but most of the players are relatively unenthusiastic and convinced it's a lost cause. In addition, some off the court issues have created intense conflict among several of the players. It seems a hot (and opportunistic) little thing named Angie decided it would be fun to date a pro ball player. Problem is, she didn't stop with one but ended up dating several of the players on Coach Johnson's team, which resulted in some pretty intense jealousy and competition. Unfortunately, the ensuing drama had spilled over on to the court and was resulting in poor performance.

The defeat was humiliating. Coach Johnson's team looked like the warm up team against their much more talented and focused opponent. Their best loss was still by 12 points. Following the close of the series the players couldn't scatter quickly enough to their various pre-planned destinations.

As a result none of them were around when the announcement came down that Coach Johnson was being replaced as coach. Some of the players were sad to see him go but only a few even called to express their condolences. The general sentiment was

"Maybe we can finally get a coach that will help us win." A number of the team were traded off in an announced restructuring by the General Manager.

Team Jackson

Coach Jackson's team had a mediocre year but made the playoffs. They were happy to not be left out again and most of the players considered the season a success before they even played game one of the playoffs. Better yet, their first round opponent was pretty mediocre as well. They had actually split games 2-2 so they felt they had a good chance of winning some games if not actually taking round one.

Most of the players talked a pretty good game about doing well in the playoffs but this was not reflected in their behavior. Many players were still late to meetings, seemed to be half hearted in practice, didn't take advantage of extra opportunities, and mostly talked about non-basketball topics when they were "off the clock".

Coach Jackson was really fired up and split his time between "encouragement" and cajoling. He wanted some enthusiasm out of his team and seemed intent on using whatever means necessary to get it including threats and bribery. There were a lot of behind the scenes conversations that included words like "Do this for me and I will see that...", or "If I don't see some improvement out of you I will make sure you never...".

The playoffs started off decently but after evening up the series at 2 and 2 the series went south for Coach Jackson's team. Their opponent seemed a little more intent on winning and took the remaining games. Once they started pulling ahead, Coach Jackson's team just didn't seem to have the heart to rally no matter how badly he wanted them to.

The season ended abruptly with a 101 to 78 loss. Coach Jackson's team looked flat in the last two games and the couple of players who really wanted to win just couldn't generate momentum. Coach Jackson kept his job but he could already tell that internal support from his players was very shaky.

Several of the better players were, off the record, instructing their agents to pursue any available trade options.

Team Tenley

Coach Tenley's team gathered for their not regularly scheduled team meeting. There was great excitement in the air as their play-off opponent had been determined from the game the night before. Their opponent was tough and recognized in the league as a really good play off team. Coach Tenley's team also recognized that they had played well that year and had some good momentum going into the playoffs having won 7 of their last 10 games against some pretty stout opponents. By now the players were used to these "extra" called meetings and had come to look forward to the opportunity to plan, strategize, and trouble shoot any challenges.

Coach Tenley was silent for a bit and the room became so quiet you could have heard a pin drop. Finally he broke out in a huge grin and said, "We're here." The room erupted in applause and celebration as the players high fived each other. Eventually the room settled down and Coach Tenley spoke again. "Let's do that again after we win the title." Players grinned and winked at each other. "But for now, its time to get down to work! We have a pretty tough opponent in this first round. Fortunately we have the talent and dedication to send them packing!"

Coach Tenley then began to unpack his plan for taking on their worthy opponent. It was a masterpiece of intricacy and yet fundamentally simple. It was obviously the result of multiple hours of reviewing tape. Many of the team members had also done their homework, keeping detailed notes on previous games, reviewing tape, etc. They brought their own ideas, which, Coach Tenley eagerly accepted. By the time the meeting was over all the players had their assignments and knew where they had to focus their energy in the coming days. They made some commitments to each other about how to prepare, one of the team member's ideas, and ended the meeting in a tight circle with a moment of silent reflection.

When game one of the playoffs arrived Coach Tenley's team was ready mentally, physically, attitudinally, and fully committed to their collective plan. The locker room was electric as the team prepared to take the court. Coach Tenley ran through a few last minute pointers then paused. The silence seemed to last longer than the actual 15 seconds. "I am so incredibly proud of you," he said earnestly. "You earned this, and there is not a finer group of men I would rather go to battle with...now let's go kick some ass!" The collective energy in the room finally converged into one combined enthusiastic shout. Chests bumped, fists pumped, and hearts soared. It was game time!

Coach Tenley's team went deep into the playoffs. Though challenged multiple times they always seemed to muster that extra push to drive forward and startle their opponents. They were on fire. When one part of the team faltered there seemed to be an endless line of those ready to step in and reignite success. Though they did not win the championship they did get to the finals and push them to a breathtaking 7th game. Losing by just 3 points was both disappointing and inspiring. On the one hand, they were thrilled with how far they had come in one season. On the other hand, they couldn't wait to begin planning to actually win the championship the following year!

Questions:

- How prepared is each team for victory? Defeat?

- How important is attitude in going into a big event?

- Why do some teams/individuals seem to give up at the first sign of trouble while others push through to victory?

- How well does your team handle victory? Defeat?

NOTES

_____
_____
_____
_____
_____
_____
_____
_____
_____
_____
_____
_____
_____
_____
_____
_____
_____
_____
_____
_____
_____
_____
_____

Why when I ask for a pair of hands do I get a brain?

– Henry Ford

Toyota gets on average 40 suggestion a year from every employee.

CONCLUSION

Fictional? Yes. Manufactured? No! The attitudes represented by these teams, individual players, and coaches are reflective of attitudes and behaviors expressed in companies and organizations on a daily basis.

This brief teaching tale is intended to spark both individual contributors and managers to consider the benefits and value of working from shared vision and goals vs. a top down driven agenda.

After hearing very negative ratings about his management team a supervisor remarked it was because "Grown men don't like to be told what to do." My response was, "Exactly! So stop telling grown men what to do."

I believe real money is left on the table in a command and control approach in which mandates are handed down from on high. I worked for a company where production increases were dreamed up overseas and then communicated down through the many layers of leadership. By the time the "We need to increase production by 12%" trickled to the factory floor the response was "Whatever". Imagine a different conversation that started on the factory floor with a question like, "How much do you believe we are capable of increasing production and what would we have to do to get there?" It would spark a conversation about both barriers and opportunities and if done right might result in a production increase that far exceeded 12%! You would also have buy in at the lowest level!

Collaboration may seem like more work on the front end but it ends up being less work in the long run and yields more lasting results.